VERSUS VIRUS

THE SILENT PANDEMIC THAT IS DESTROYING THE WORLD

HERMAN DEBOARD III
Organizational Communication Specialist

11664 National Blvd, #345
Los Angeles, CA. 90064
310-584-1504
www.TVGuestpertPublishing.com
www.TVGuestpert.com
First Printing 2023
10 9 8 7 6 5 4 3 2 1

TABLE OF CONTENTS

I f the World needs a vaccine… it is for the Versus Virus. What is the Versus Virus, you might ask? It's a silent killer of individuality. It is a virus that attacks both the biological and psychological systems in your body and works to turn you into a supercarrier destined to spread the Virus to everyone you come in contact with.

It's a virus that exploits your innate need for belonging and manipulates you into erasing your identity and assimilating to the control of "The Team".

That's right… you have assimilated into a "Team Think" organism and have, for the most part, given up your right to be a free-thinking individual. It's time to identify this virus in your system and seek it out to destroy it once and for all.

My name is Herman DeBoard, and I am an odd mixture of the social and physical scientist. After spending thirteen years in the military and the federal government, I returned to school to complete my bachelor's degree and master's degree in communication studies. After this, I went on to earn my Ph.D. in Education where I focused on Adult Learning Methodologies. I took this path because I had a strong desire to learn both how people communicate effectively and how people learn. I am now studying Physics in my spare time and believe this multidisciplinary approach to learning has given me a broader perspective on life and humanity.

I am writing this book in a self-help format. First, to help people try and understand what the Versus Virus is and how it is impacting everyday life, including relationships. Second, I want to provide a few tools that can act as a mental vaccination to help you defeat the virus impacting your mind and body once and for all. This is meant to be a quick read that I hope will make an immense impact on your life. Let's get enlightened together.

SYMPTOMS OF THE VERSUS VIRUS

I have called this a "virus" which means it has to have symptoms. How else will you know if you have it? I took the time to do a small independent study of my friends and social media followers where I simply interviewed them online to try and isolate the symptoms of the virus that, I believe, is destroying the world as we know it. It is important to note that I am not a medical doctor, nor am I a psychiatrist or psychologist. I am a social scientist and an expert in human communication and adult learning methodologies. What I am writing here falls directly in line with my personal area of expertise, my personal experiences, and the experiences of those people whom I have interviewed and surveyed.

SYMPTOM 1: Uncontrollable anger or agitation when discussing hot topics

The Versus Virus can be a debilitating condition that can negatively impact the lives of those who are infected. One common symptom includes anger or agitation when discussing hot topics in both small and large groups. Basically, your thoughts and feelings have been manipulated to the boiling point and you have lost the ability to have a debate on topics you consider "hot." These can topics such as politics, race, gender, education, sports, parenting, the critical race theory (CRT), and many others.

What is important to understand is that we live in an era of information overload, where most of that information is inaccurate, misleading, or just plain propaganda designed to persuade or dissuade you into developing a belief system based on the information I mention here.

Let's take news media as an example. Most people that I interviewed and surveyed choose a media station based on their own belief system, even if that belief system has been poorly formed. They are simply looking for confirmation of their beliefs. This is known as "confirmation bias." My interpretation of the surveys that I conducted basically tells me that we, as consumers of media, engage with the news to inform ourselves and we tend to put a great deal of trust and credibility in the news media sources that we choose to consume. While we want to believe that the news media and the personalities we see are balanced, fair and accurate, it is a very gray area as it pertains to the underlying motivations of stories published on any network. In this example, when your bias about a topic is confirmed by a group you have given trust to, it only exacerbates the agitation when someone you come in contact with has a different viewpoint than yourself or your trusted sources.

SYMPTOM 2: Avoidance of friends and family

The Versus Virus can infiltrate the very essence of who you are while manipulating your thoughts to the point that you believe your friends and family have turned against you. When this happens, you start to avoid gatherings of any size because you believe the very presence of the people there will trigger you and increase your overall anxiety levels. This is directly related to symptom 1, uncontrollable agitation or anger.

One quick question I would challenge you with is, are your beliefs surrounding hot topics like politics, sports, the environment, etc., more important than the human relationships in your life? We will come back to this later in the book.

SYMPTOM 3: Unfollowing and unfriending people on social media

The Versus Virus has taken over your personality and your idea of self when you can't even scroll through social media without certain posts or people triggering you to the point that your cortisol levels and anxiety start to bubble up.

This issue has progressively become more intense year over year, as social influencers that you may have given your trust to are encouraging you to pick the side that they follow and completely ostracize, or attack anyone who doesn't follow the same line of thinking.

SYMPTOM 4: Avoidance of hot topic conversations in any public gathering

For many individuals with the Versus Virus, Hot Topic conversations can be a significant trigger. Discussing hot topics can often evoke intense emotions such as anger and fear which can exacerbate symptoms of the Versus Virus. This means that people living with the condition may struggle to take part in conversations about current events or engage in debates and dialogues around political topics.

While there are other symptoms I am uncovering, the shocking part of this mini study to me was that 100% of everyone I spoke to have some sort of the virus symptoms listed here. And most of them had no idea they had become infected and that it was negatively impacting their personal lives.

Let's start to break down the root of the Versus Virus.

CHAPTER ONE

TEAMS ARE EVERYWHERE

To understand why I use the word "versus" in the title, you need to grasp the concept of teams. When you see two different teams on a sports field, they are against, or versus, each other. Whether you know it or not, you are on at least a dozen teams and potentially many more. The choices you make in everyday life decide the teams you are on. You choose viewpoints, or beliefs on various topics in your life, that are important to you like pro-choice vs. pro-life, to get vaccines or not to get vaccines, or gun control vs. the 2nd amendment… right down to an NFL game of the Broncos vs. the Cowboys. And every single one of these groups are a team with unique leaders, strategies, and *manipulation tactics*.

From the moment you opened your eyes, you were on team blue, team pink, or team green or purple. This was already decided by your parents, not by you. You are on teams that represent your religion or lack thereof, your hometown, and your school, even your taste in music places you on a team. Think punk, rocker, or goth. Then as you get older, you join bigger teams that represent your political beliefs, and you move into communities that represent your socio-economic teams. Right down to the clothes you wear and the things you eat and drink, all places you on a team. If you think this is a silly notion, just walk into any room and start talking to a random group of people about their diet. You will instantly start a discussion about why you should be a vegan, or on a plant-based diet, or why keto and eating protein is the team you should be on. You will even get people saying they are on the "eat whatever you want in moderation team."

Let's look at religion, as well. Most of us got our religious teachings from our parents. Right out of the womb, we could be faith-based people or atheists. Then consider that there are sub-teams of faith based. You could be on Team Christian, Team Islam, Team Hindu, Team Buddhist, or Team Judaism. Even these major groups have sub-teams. For example, there are around 300 denominations of Christianity. All of them believe they have a better team than the others.

Everything you have ever bought, said, or posted on social media has been influenced by a team you have chosen to be on and has become a part of your persona that tells the world what team colors you are flying. Whether you know it or not, your teams identify who you are… and they just might be controlling your thought process which is ultimately eating away at your individuality. And that… has become the worst virus ever unleashed on the world.

CHAPTER TWO

INDIVIDUALITY & MOTIVATIONS

We live in a world where very few people still have control of their individuality. In the United States, we are supposed to live in a free society where individual freedoms are valued and protected. But with the over 100 people that I interviewed in writing this book, 97% of them could not explain to me "why" they believe what they believe. When pressed, it was because "someone they followed as a leader told them to believe this." They had essentially joined a team and were taking orders from a coach whom they knew nothing about concerning the coach or leader's motivations or who the coach or leader's own influences might have been.

While I will get into the role of the coach a little later in this book, I will simply ask a few questions now to plant the seeds. Who are the coaches or leaders that you allow to influence your thoughts and behaviors? And what are their motivations? Do you even know? And do you know who your coach's coaches are or were? Who has influenced them to think the way they do and what were their motivations? All of these questions are extremely important if you want to truly be free from the Versus Virus.

And as an added layer of awareness, every team you are on is using proven psychological methods to further gain your loyalty and trust. From applying psychological principles to their copywriting, to using certain colors that evoke emotion, to using tactics like social proof and the decoy effect, every team is looking to increase your loyalty to them, that is ultimately infecting you with the Versus Virus. Social proof is, by definition, "a psychological phenomenon where people assume the actions of others in an attempt to reflect correct behavior for a given situation. In essence, it's the notion that, since others are doing it, I should be doing it, too." (*https://www.dynamicyield.com/glossary/social-proof/*). The other tactic, the decoy effect, "describes how, when we are choosing between two alternatives, the addition of a third, less attractive option (the decoy) can influence our perception of the original two choices." (*https://thedecisionlab.com/biases/decoy-effect*)

As we go forward here in a deep dive, keep the words *individuality and motivations* in the back of your mind as these are the two biggest concepts I want you to take away after reading this book.

CHAPTER THREE

TEAMS

S o, the virus that has grown to pandemic proportions attacks the very heart of your individuality and turns you into a supercarrier... wandering the world and spreading the virus without even knowing what you are doing. Let's look at some very high-profile examples of what I mean by this statement.

POLITICAL TEAMS: Politics Are Everywhere

Chances are, if you bought this book, you are of the age where you are on one or more Political Teams. Politics are everywhere. They are in everything we watch for entertainment, everything we listen to, and everything we wear, eat, or drive. Everything in society has an underlying political message. Disney is changing classic movie characters to support the message of diversity. Public schools, colleges, and universities are changing their grading and evaluation process all in the name of equity. Even social media companies go out of their way to promote political messages they deem as important while censoring messages they may not agree with. Politics are everywhere.

It's important to note that as you read through these examples, I am personally not taking any sort of side whatsoever. I am simply identifying that the teams exist and that they are indeed manipulating you in many unhealthy ways. I have recognized the impact this Versus Virus has had on my decisions and social relationships and have taken the necessary steps to identify the teams I was on and remove myself to see the world from a clearer perspective. Once you go through his process, you will equate it to sitting in a chair in front of Morpheus while he offers you the blue pill or the red pill. Even as I type that metaphor, I am very aware that even that movie scene has been politicized and weaponized.

Team Liberal Versus Team Conservative

Team Liberal vs. Team Conservative might be the most common two political teams around the world. Setting aside a few countries that do not legally allow freedom of choice politically, most countries allow you to choose between two or three different parties of political thought. Normally, these groups, no matter what they are called formally, are grouped into the Liberal thinkers on the left and the Conservative thinkers on the right. I'm going to make a few generalizations here about Liberals and Conservatives but keep an open mind as you read my descriptions. I fully understand that all Conservatives and Liberals do not believe all of the things I am writing down; but generally, this is a pretty good starting point.

Team Liberal Is Normally Referred to as "Left-Wing"

Liberal team members normally prefer things like universal health care that should be provided by the government to all citizens. They believe that the government should provide services to less fortunate people and should increase taxes if necessary. They believe that high-income earners should pay a larger percentage of their income in taxes. Socially, they believe gay couples should get equal rights, abortion should be legal, and gun ownership should be restricted. Regarding personal responsibility, Liberals normally believe that the government should provide a set structure of life and that laws should be enacted to protect everyone for an equal society, sometimes at the expense of economic and other types of freedoms.

Team Conservative Is Normally Referred to as "Right Wing"

Conservatives are said to prefer smaller governments and less regulation. They prefer that services are provided by the private sector in a free market and have a literal interpretation of the Constitution that governs the country. Economically, they believe the government should tax less and spend less. They generally believe that to balance the budget you must cut spending. They also believe that in the free market, higher-income earners should have the incentive to invest in the economy and small businesses. They also normally have conservative religious views where they oppose things like gay marriage. They normally support the right to bear arms, the death penalty, and personal responsibility as an individual. This means that each person should exercise personal responsibility and that the government's role is to hold them accountable for following the laws of the land.

In the back of your mind, I'm sure you already know which of these two teams you are on. Now let's go one step deeper. Now that we have outlined the basic identity of Team Liberal and Team Conservative, let's look at some of the sub-teams inside each.

Team Woke Versus Team Anti-Woke

These two teams are very interesting to me and, hopefully, they will be to you as well. Team Liberal generally takes the term "woke" to represent a term of endearment, and believes it means that a person is aware of racial discrimination and other forms of oppression and injustice. They also tend to believe that if you are not woke, you are leaning more toward racist or elitist standards concerning your thoughts and behaviors.

Team Conservative, on the other side of the aisle, believes that woke is a negative term that stands reality on its head. They believe that it means the opposite of reality and that someone is woke to "fantasies and daydreams" that have nothing to do with reality at all.

One thing you should know about me is that even though I was an accomplished athlete in high school, college, and in the military, I have always been active on the Speech and Debate Team at every school I attended. Debate involves formal discussion on a topic. In a debate, arguments are presented to persuade or dissuade others on the point you are arguing. So, I am a staunch advocate of spirited yet respectful debate. But when I interview people who proudly claim to be on Team Liberal or Team Conservative, or on Team Woke or Team Anti-Woke, all respect and ability to reason seems to go out the door. And the most fascinating part of what I have observed is that only a very small percentage of people on these teams can give validated factual information about why they are on the team they are on and why they dislike the members of the other team. They are, for all intents and purposes, infected with the dreaded Versus Virus.

And again, what makes the impacts of this negative on your intrapersonal self is that you are more than likely allowing leaders from these teams to manipulate your beliefs even further, which can inflame the symptoms I mentioned earlier in this book.

With that in mind, let's continue looking at other teams on the hot topics list that you are potentially on.

Team Pro-Choice vs. Team Pro-Life

Now let's look at an even hotter topic… abortion. The Versus Virus has infected these two teams to their core, to the point that many literally hate each other. People have lost the ability to have constructive dialogue around the topic and often have resorted to verbal and, sometimes, physical attacks against outspoken members of the opposing team. We see this topic on all types of mainstream and social media including protests, shootings, bombings, and more.

The abortion debate has been a heated topic of discussion for decades. On one side, you have those who think it's an essential medical procedure that should be accessible to all; on the other side, some believe it goes against their moral and religious beliefs. No matter which team you are on, one thing is certain: this isn't going away anytime soon!

When it comes to debating abortion, it seems like everyone has something to say—and they're not afraid to shout it from the rooftops. So, buckle up, because no matter which way the wind blows, the abortion debate is sure to keep us talking for years to come. Who knows? Maybe someday we'll find some common ground and come to a consensus on this complicated issue. Until then, take a breath, because the debate is only getting started!

And, as I am sure you know already, these teams are also ingrained as sub-teams inside Team Liberal (pro) and Team Conservative (against). Now you have multiple leaders from multiple teams telling you why you should believe what you do and also telling you why you should not like anyone with an opposing viewpoint.

As a reflection of this point in the book, which of these two teams do you believe you are on concerning the topic of abortion? And ask yourself if this topic and your beliefs on the topic are so important to you that you dislike anyone who disagrees with you.

Team Gun Control vs. Team 2nd Amendment

All the previous examples lead to one of the hottest topics and two of the most divided teams in the world, especially in the United States, where the actual Constitution protects citizens' rights to keep and bear arms.

Team Gun Control uses current events like school shootings and nightclub shootings to support their belief that gun ownership should be restricted by the government.

Team 2nd Amendment tends to hold the Constitution up as law showing that it is there to protect citizens against the overreach of the federal government.

The gun control debate is a heated one, with passionate advocates and opponents on either Team. But here's the thing: both sides can agree that we need to find a way to reduce gun violence in our society. While I am not taking sides on this or any topic I write about in this book, I will provide my humble opinions sporadically. Specifically, in regard to how these two groups might start a dialogue for understanding, I believe that starts by recognizing that there are responsible and law-abiding gun owners out there who respect their Second Amendment rights, as well as those working to protect the public from unnecessary risks related to firearms. It's time for a compromise between these two camps so that we can create sensible laws that reduce gun crime without infringing on an individual's right to bear arms.

The problem lies in the fact that the debate is so heated that neither Team wants to truly listen to the valid arguments from the other side. They are infected with the Versus Virus. Have you given any thought to which of these teams you may be on?

NON-POLITICAL TEAMS

Not every team you are on appears to be as controversial as the examples given earlier. It doesn't mean they are not a part of the Versus Virus that is attacking the very essence of your mind and body. Let's look at a few of these.

Geographic Teams

The country, state, city, and town where you were born or where you currently choose to reside has quickly become a part of the Versus Virus.

Have you ever felt a surge of pride for your country? Whether your part of the United States, Canada, England, France, China or any other nation around the world, there's something special about having an allegiance to a place that's yours.

No matter where life takes us, we can always come back home and find solace in our corner of the world. You don't have to be an international traveler to feel connected with your homeland. Simply looking at its flag is enough to make anyone who is a citizen swell with national pride!

From a country standpoint, look at the US versus China. Relations have broken down over the past few years and the sides seem to have lost the ability to have diplomatic conversations about working together. US-China relations have been a rollercoaster ride. Times of engagement, mistrust, and everything in between have characterized the tumultuous two decades of diplomatic ties between these two superpowers. From trade wars to diplomatic meetings, it's hard not to take notice of the dynamic relationship between these two countries. It almost seems like they are magnets—no matter how hard they try to keep away from each other, something pulls them back together!

In looking at their stance against each other, these two sides are obviously different teams where the members of the two teams are made up of both naturalized citizens as well as supporters of both countries internationally.

And then there is Russia versus Ukraine where an actual war is being fought between Teams (or countries). The Russia-Ukraine war has been a continuing source of tension in the region since 2014. After Russian troops annexed the Crimean Peninsula, the conflict between the two nations escalated to include military action in Eastern Ukraine. Over 10,000 people have been killed and at least 1.5 million displaced as a result of the war and its aftermath. Residents, who have been caught in the middle of the conflict, suffer from a lack of access to basic services and infrastructure damage due to fighting. The war has also had a detrimental impact on the economy of Ukraine, with an estimated annual loss of 3-5% GDP growth. Despite numerous international peace initiatives, little progress has been made toward a resolution to the conflict.

Now people around the world are being asked to pick a team. Are you Team Ukraine or Team Russia? Why did you choose this side? Do you actually know what they are fighting over? Or have you formed an opinion and joined a team just because an influencer told you to?

Team Patriotism

When you live in a country, the majority of citizens in that country are on Team Country. This is sometimes referred to as Team Patriotism. But in recent years, countries have become split, where the very word "Patriotism" is being weaponized as a Team in itself. The Versus Virus has split the population into patriotic vs. unpatriotic.

Patriotism is a powerful emotion that has motivated many people to stand up and defend their countries. For citizens of Ukraine, patriotism has become an especially motivating factor amidst the ongoing conflict with Russia. Ukrainian volunteers have joined the fight against Russian-backed forces in Eastern Ukraine, while others have rallied behind humanitarian efforts or taken part in protests and demonstrations in support of Ukraine. This patriotism is not a sign of aggression, but rather an affirmation of the right to self-determination and national sovereignty. It serves as a reminder that we must continue to strive for peace and an end to the conflict between Ukraine and Russia. Only then will both nations be able to move forward and build a brighter future together.

Patriotism in the United States, however, is being weaponized between the two major political parties. Being a Patriot has come to mean you are on the conservative team where you are possibly labeled as a racist while being anti-patriotic has come to be a part of the liberal team where you may have some negative feelings toward your own country.

The very fact that you can watch this word as it takes on different meanings in different countries should make you stand up and take notice. After you do your research, you may decide to choose a team, or you may decide to remove yourself from either team altogether. Your mental health may depend on it. One glaring point I would like to bring light to is that nowhere in the description of these two teams is Team Peace or Team Diplomacy. Every team we are on, including the two of these is promoting animosity toward the other team, which, in the long run, is potentially negatively impacting your mental health.

Now, let's break this geographic team category down into sub-teams. You have either chosen to live in the state or province where you currently reside, or you have made the choice to start the process of relocating to a state that feels more like the team you are supposed to be on. The news has been very open about reporting the great migration of citizens who were formerly living in states like New York and California, but who made the conscious choice to move themselves and their businesses to states like Texas or Florida. These decisions seem to be made based on business opportunities, taxation, and other policies and laws passed in the states. No matter the reason, these people have essentially switched teams. So, before we move on to the next section… ask yourself if you currently believe the majority of the policies and laws your current state is laying out for its citizens are the ones you agree with.

Religious Teams

Religion is a curious topic as it pertains to the Versus Virus. Just look at the number of deaths caused by religious conflicts worldwide. Some of the deadliest religious conflicts in history include the Crusades which resulted in 6 million deaths, the Thirty Years' War which resulted in 11.5 million deaths, the French Wars of Religion which resulted in 4 million deaths and the Muslim Conquests of India which resulted in 80 million deaths. Being on a religious team of any kind seems to make one dislike all other religious teams. These numbers represent the Versus Virus hard at work.

Muslims Versus Christians

Muslims and Christians are two of the world's largest religions, and they have significant differences in their beliefs and practices. While many people recognize these differences as a source of debate or disagreement, it is important to remember that both faiths share common values like love, compassion, justice, mercy, and service to humanity. Despite having different interpretations of scripture and theological practices, each faith ultimately seeks to bring peace and harmony into the world through its teachings. The key is for believers from both sides to seek understanding rather than animosity between them. Through mutual respect and understanding, we can bridge gaps between our communities despite our differing viewpoints. We must strive for peaceful coexistence rather than dwelling on disagreements to create a better future for all of us.

And while I type this, it is easy to turn on any news station to hear of violent conflicts going on between Muslim and Christian groups. So, as you continue to read, take note of whether you are on a religious team and if you have strong negative feelings about other types of religions. If the answer is yes, then ask yourself where those negative beliefs came from and try to get to an understanding in your own mind that will reduce or eliminate the negativity created by the Versus Virus.

Palestinians Versus Jews

There is the major, decades-old conflict between Israel and Palestine. The Israeli–Palestinian conflict goes back to the late 19th and early 20th centuries. Stemming from nationalist movements among the Jews and the Arabs, both teams were set on attaining sovereignty for their team members in the Middle East.

This century-old war essentially started and continues because of a land dispute between two different religions, which each believes they have the sole right to the "holy land" in between them.

This is yet another set of religious teams that many people, who do not even live in the region, have decided to join. You can go to any country and ask people about this conflict, and you will quickly understand if they are on Team Israel or Team Palestine.

SOCIETAL ISSUE TEAMS

Team White Versus Team Black

Next, I want to go through a few of the Societal Issue Teams. These can represent issues such as Team Black vs. Team White, which always makes me question why all the other colors in between have been left out. The long history of racial injustice in the United States has resulted in deep divisions between many black and white people when it comes to political issues. From civil rights legislation to the criminal justice system to voting rights, the disparities between how African Americans and other minorities are treated compared to their white counterparts are reportedly stark.

The big issue here is that you now have two very distinct teams that have formed, and there is a very high probability that anyone you talk to is on one of the teams. Oddly enough, I can't refer to these teams as Team Black or Team White because people of every culture and color have joined and not at all based on their skin color. There are light skinned people on Team Black and there are dark skinned people on Team White. But the central idea I want you to understand here is that there are leaders from these groups whose singular purpose is to manipulate you into joining their team and disliking anyone who is on the other team. It's all about division, because if there is division, then someone is gaining more power.

The first team, Team White, believes that bad things happened in history, but great strides have been taken to rid the world of these racist policies. They further believe that everyone in modern society has the same chance at success as anyone else, and it's the media that is propagating the divisive issue of racism in the population. This team is made up of people of all colors, including both black and white.

The second team, Team Black, is a team that strongly believes these racial inequalities are still going on in American society and in other countries. Many members of this team are still fighting for reparations to be paid based on historical acts of slavery. This team is also made up of people of all colors including both black and white.

You can talk to any person you run into and the majority of them have chosen a team to be on for this topic. Take a moment to make a note of which team you have chosen. And as you consider your stance, I would encourage you to expand your research to countries other than the United States.

If you really want to see modern-day slavery and oppression in action, there are dozens of countries where this is going on at an alarming rate, and it has nothing to do with black versus white. According to the US State Department, modern slavery mainly falls into the categories of sex trafficking and forced labor. (*https://www.state.gov/what-is-modern-slavery/*) All I am asking of my readers is to simply open your mind, gather all of the evidence… and then make your choice.

Team Electric Versus Team Fossil Fuel

The electric car versus fossil fuel debate has been ongoing for many years. The introduction of electric cars into the mainstream market has seen a shift in public opinion towards more sustainable transportation. This is primarily due to their environmental benefits, such as lower emissions, reduced air pollution, and improved energy efficiency. However, this does not come without its own set of issues; electric cars are expensive to buy and maintain, require charging infrastructure for longer journeys, and have a limited range before needing to be recharged. Moreover, the electricity generation still relies heavily on fossil fuels and non-renewable sources of energy making it difficult for some countries or regions to make the switch to electric vehicles in an economically viable manner.

Despite these drawbacks, the development of new technologies such as renewable energy sources and battery storage could help to reduce the impact of electric cars on the environment and make them a more viable option for many. As such, the debate continues as governments and industry leaders strive to find a balance between cost, sustainability, convenience, and safety. Ultimately, it remains to be seen which type of vehicle will come out on top in this debate.

Most people have chosen a team to be on in this category. You are either Team Fossil Fuel or you are Team Electric Car.

Team Climate Change Versus Team Natural Earth Cycles

The discussion of electric vehicles versus fossil fuels is a natural lead-in to Team Climate Change versus Team Natural Earth Cycles. The climate change debate has engaged the public for decades. On one side, there are those who believe that human activity is causing detrimental changes to the Earth's climate and ecosystems; while on the other side, there are those who argue that natural fluctuations in the Earth's climate are responsible for any observed changes.

Proponents of human-caused climate change point out that higher concentrations of greenhouse gases in the atmosphere trap heat that would otherwise escape into space. This rise in global average temperature leads to an array of consequences including ocean acidification, melting glaciers, rising sea levels, and more frequent extreme weather events. In response to this evidence, they advocate a transition away from fossil fuels towards renewable energy sources as well as investing in technologies such as carbon capture and sequestration.

Those who dispute these conclusions cite natural causes for climate change including changes in the Earth's orbit, volcanic activity, and the collection and release of CO_2 by the oceans. They argue that predictions of future climate trends are unreliable and claim that increased levels of atmospheric CO_2 will have a beneficial effect on plant growth. As an alternative to transitioning away from fossil fuels, they advocate the use of nuclear energy as it produces no emissions during operation.

In an article from the Brookings Institution, they reported, "As the world burns, a growing radical flank of the climate movement has taken to the streets in protest. Activists are blocking traffic, marching slowly, smearing paint, throwing food, and disrupting events to bring attention to the climate crisis and the need for more aggressive climate action." These "radical flanks" are indeed infected by the Versus Virus to the point of aggression.

Team Vax Versus Team Choice

The debate over mandatory vaccines versus personal health choices has garnered significant attention in recent years. At the core of this issue is a tension between the need for public health and individual rights to self-determination. On one hand, vaccines are an essential tool in protecting public health by preventing the spread of disease and illness. Proponents of mandatory vaccination argue that it serves as a safeguard against outbreaks, particularly among vulnerable populations such as young children, who cannot receive vaccinations due to their age or medical condition. On the other hand, opponents of mandatory vaccination assert that individuals should have control over their own bodies and personal choices when it comes to healthcare decisions. They point out that while some may benefit from mandated immunizations, others may be at risk of adverse effects from the vaccine.

Ultimately, an individual's stance on this issue comes down to a personal decision and is based on many factors, including religious or philosophical beliefs regarding medical treatments, prior experiences with vaccinations, and an understanding of the potential risks associated with each one. Citizens and lawmakers alike need to keep in mind that when it comes to matters of health choice versus mandated vaccines, there is no one-size-fits-all solution.

Again, without me personally taking a side here, I can say

from an organizational communication expert's educated opinion that both approaches should be taken into consideration to ensure everyone has access to safe and effective preventative care while preserving the right of individuals to make informed decisions about their own healthcare needs. No matter the debate, chances are that you have chosen to be on one of these teams. I would only ask that you try to use critical thinking skills and a little empathy for the other side before engaging in heated or spirited debates.

Team Censorship Versus Team Free Speech

Now we come to what I believe is one of the strangest two Societal Issue Teams that surfaced over the past few years, Team Censorship versus Team Free Speech. Team Censorship believes that Team Free Speech should be censored for saying things that go against Team Censorships beliefs, and Team Free Speech believes that all voices should be heard no matter if you agree with them or not. Also, what I've seen trending is that Team Liberal seems to have adopted Team Censorship as their own, while Team Conservative takes ownership of Team Free Speech.

When discussing censorship versus free speech, we must recognize that the argument does not currently apply to all countries as some have laws against freedoms including free speech. In the United States where I reside, freedom of speech is a cornerstone of democracy and an essential human right that is listed in the United States Constitution and outlined in the First Amendment. It allows people to express their ideas without fear of retribution or censorship from the government. Without this freedom, I would not be allowed to write this book, as it is questioning the motivation of many institutions in our country.

Team Censorship seems to be arguing that censorship can be a necessary tool in certain cases. For example, during the COVID campaigns of 2021 and 2022, Team Censorship argued that governments should impose restrictions on certain kinds of speech to protect national security or public safety. They also argued that some forms of speech that they deemed as hateful or non-inclusive should be tagged and labeled in public and thus subject to censorship. We are currently seeing the evidence of this censorship activity play out on television as the Twitter (now known simply as X) File Trials are in progress in the United States Senate.

In the argument between these two teams, when you strike away all of the name-calling and anger between the two sides, what you are left with at the root is the issue of "Civil Liberties."

Freedom of Speech is, in the United States, a Civil Liberty for all. Currently the two teams have formed and Team Liberal, who adopted Team Censorship as their own, has decided they want to end Civil Liberty for all that is Free Speech. But what happens when the power shifts back to Team Conservative and you have fought to remove this important Civil Liberty? Now you are the one being censored.

It is only through an informed and thoughtful approach that we can get to an agreement between these two strange teams. And again, there is a very strong chance that you have chosen one of these teams to be on.

Team Socioeconomic Status

In addition to all the teams mentioned here, there are also Socioeconomic Teams. This is where people have been placed in teams based on an economic status defined by society and based on the amount of income they earn in a given year. This can lead to teams such as Team Poverty, Team Lower Class, Team Middle Class, or Team Upper Class. These groups are used as pawns by major political groups who seek to persuade them to vote them into power based on campaign promises. You may not have chosen to be on a team in this category, but you are on one.

The major difference here is that you may not see obvious leaders of Team Middle Class. What you will see instead are other teams, such as Team Liberal or Team Conservative, who are manipulating these groups to put them into power so they can make positive changes for their group. In the manipulations, they will try to convince team members that the other groups are holding them back and that if you put them in power, they will get you what you deserve. This has been going on for centuries as a tactic to control major populations of people.

Team Education Versus Team Parent

When you think of Team Education, you might think of attending a school—you like your teachers, you cheer for the sports teams, and you have some school pride. You want your school to win academic awards, games, and tournaments and to be the best school there is. But what happens when your school's educational policies become political, and you find that their policies have created a team that is competing against them? This has happened in the past couple of years and has created a new opposing team I am calling Team Parent.

For example, many schools have decided to drop qualification exams such as the SAT and they are dropping final exams in general because of equity. Many schools are starting to implement programs like the critical race theory into the curriculum, which schools are fully allowed to do as independent institutions. But this has upset many people on Team Parent who would like schools to focus on education and leave social issues up to them. Instead of just flying your school's colors, you are now presented with multiple policy-based teams that could make you be against your school in the end.

To understand if this has happened at your Alma Mater, simply do some research to find out if they have been in the news recently for any of the issues I have listed in this book. And if you find any of these issues do come up, then ask yourself which side of the argument you stand on. This will be the team in which you have allowed yourself to be placed.

Team Transgender Athletes Versus Team Women's Sports

The controversy surrounding transgender athletes in

women's sports has been a hot topic for some time. Team Transgender Athlete argues that transgender athletes should be allowed to compete in sports based on the gender identity they identify with, while Team Women's Sports counter that they pose an unfair advantage due to inherent physiological differences between men and women and that only biological women should compete with other biological women.

The issue has become increasingly politicized in recent years due to the growing transgender participation in sports and news coverage, and particularly as countries, governing programs and some US states have begun introducing legislation to restrict or limit the participation of trans athletes in female sporting events. The conversation is complicated by medical considerations, as not all transgender individuals medically transition through hormone therapies, and there are still questions of how best to categorize those whose physical or hormonal characteristics do not fit into traditional definitions of male or female genders.

Again, just turning on the television or bringing this topic up at dinner will most likely spark a lively debate and will all but force you to pick a side and join a team. Which team have you decided to be on?

Media Teams

Media Teams might be the most prolific transmitter of the Versus Virus in the world. Media Teams include Mainstream Media outlets like CNN, MSNBC, Fox News, or BBC News. They include television, radio, print, and internet outlets of all kinds. Media outlets pick a team based on their leadership (coaches) and their sponsors (boosters). They then work tirelessly to discredit the teams that they are against, many times paying no attention to facts or making vague misrepresentations of the facts in general. Their goal is seemingly to persuade or dissuade viewers on topics that are important to their organization, including the companies who pay their bills.

By choosing one of these outlets as "your team," you are giving them the power to manipulate your thoughts and behaviors more than any other set of organizations on the planet. The funny thing is, as I interviewed people to gather information for this book, I found out that most people define a "News Organization" as a group of unbiased investigative journalists. The reality in which we live could not be more different.

It is not my goal to tear these organizations down. It is my intention, however, to identify to the world that this is going on in hopes that the organizations might one day use true critical thinking skills to stop this harmful spreading of the Versus Virus and one day become a true investigative journalistic organization that supports the concepts of debate and critical thinking. This could be one of the largest contributors to mental health issues on the Earth, but further studies will have to be done to show a real correlation.

CHAPTER FOUR

PSYCHOLOGY OF TEAMS

N ow that you understand what I mean by "team" and you have seen the obvious teams that the world is trying to force you to be a part of, let's take a deep dive into the psychology behind teams in general.

THE ORIGIN OF TEAMS

Teams have been around since the dawn of time. It's no surprise that teams are still so popular today. From early hunter-gatherer societies to modern teams at work, teams offer a powerful way for people to come together, collaborate, and make collective decisions. But what makes teams so successful? What is it about teams that resonate with us as human beings? A key factor in a team's success lies in its ability to bring out the best in each member by tapping into collective wisdom and resources. By leveraging the strengths of each individual, teams can achieve much more than any one person could accomplish on their own. So, teams may have been around for centuries, but they're still as relevant today as ever before!

Ultimately, teams offer something that no single individual can: the power of collective action. As a result, teams will continue to play an important role in our lives—whether it's at home, in the workplace, or out in the world. But the collective action of teams can also lead to an unhealthy "Team Mentality" that eliminates your freedom of individuality.

Team Mentality and Manipulation Tactics

We live in a competitive world driven by the desire to succeed. This is very evident when you look at the phenomenon of "influencers" and social media. More and more people have decided to become internet influencers to have the career and pay they desire.

Influencers, sports leagues, businesses, political parties, cities, countries, and entertainment acts, all build brands, or "Teams," to compete with other brands or Teams. This psychological warfare builds one team up with good feelings while tearing down other teams and by proxy, the members of those teams. Every team you are on spends thousands of hours and sometimes millions of dollars to add their team's definition to your personality. They are working overtime to tell you what you should believe and why you should believe it. They want to train you how to talk about their team through branding.

You read that correctly. All the teams you are part of work to develop your persona for you, so you don't have to think about it. This is a very well-thought-out manipulation tactic to get that Versus Virus deeper into your nervous system.

Team Politics and Manipulation Tactics

Political Parties are constantly using gaslighting tactics to psychologically manipulate you into believing what they want you to believe about a specific topic. The main concept here is if I get you on my team, you will do what I say and vote for me in the next election. I can feed you soundbites to repeat in public, tell you what colors to wear, and who to like and who to dislike. But no matter your viewpoint, this is 100% manipulation on the part of the team and is a major part of the Versus Virus that has infected your body. The key word here is manipulation.

Political manipulation is a tactic used by governments and organizations to influence public opinion and shape political outcomes. It can be used to promote certain interests while silencing opposition or to push particular policies or agendas. Political manipulation often involves misinformation, propaganda, censorship, bribery, intimidation, and other forms of coercion. In extreme cases, it can even lead to the suppression of dissent or the implementation of oppressive measures such as martial law. In some instances, political manipulation is used for personal gain rather than for the benefit of society as a whole. Unfortunately, this form of negative manipulation has become more common in recent years due to advances in technology that make it easier for governments and other actors to spread false information and manipulate public opinion with relative ease.

In the context of the Versus Virus, manipulation from any or all the teams plays a huge role in the mental health and psyche of the individual members of teams on both sides of the versus symbol that we see on the cover of this book.

Team Religion and Manipulation Tactics

Religious Sects or Denominations are constantly telling you how you should walk, talk, and behave based on their interpretation of a religious text that they have deemed as more important than other texts. This is also a very large part of the Versus Virus and makes you believe it is you against all the other teams at all costs.

Religious manipulation is a dangerous tactic that has been used for centuries to control and subjugate people, often with devastating consequences. It has been employed as a tool of control by various religions, political movements, and authorities to gain power or influence over their followers. In some cases, it involves using religious teachings or scriptures to manipulate the beliefs or behavior of individuals or groups. This can lead to oppression and even violence when those being manipulated are unable to resist its power. Religious manipulation can be seen in many forms today, including cults that use brainwashing techniques or authoritarian leaders who enforce strict rules and punishments based on religious doctrine. By manipulating the emotions and beliefs of vulnerable populations, these manipulators have caused tremendous harm throughout history.

I would like to add here that I am by no means saying that all religion is bad. Again, the underlying message of most religions is love, peace and service, but there are many fringe movements that negatively impact people by using manipulation tactics to control them. This is what you need to be watching out for.

Team Mainstream Media Manipulation Tactics

We've already established that most people have chosen a mainstream media team. No matter if that is CNN, MSNBC, or Fox News, you have made a choice.

Mainstream Media Stations are hotspots for the Versus Virus. Every single personality on Mainstream Media has an agenda to promote the views held by the company that is paying their salary, bar none. It's not their fault as they are simply being paid to be the voice of a larger corporation or team, who in turn is being paid by sponsors (boosters), or even larger teams.

Left-Wing Media personalities promote a general hatred of anyone on Team Right-Wing no matter if the story is a lie or not. And the same goes for Right-Wing Media Personalities. I call them personalities because the word journalism rarely if ever applies. Many Mainstream Media Personalities have been caught simply reading stories prepared by the networks without doing any sort of research prior to airing.

"Large numbers of people see the media as subject to undue political influence, and only a small minority believe most news organizations put what's best for society ahead of their own commercial interest," wrote Reuters Institute Director Rasmus Kleis Nielsen in a report, based on an online survey of 93,432 people, conducted in 46 markets. This was further proven in 2023 by a very viral meme-style video that showed dozens of media outlets reading the exact same story using the exact same words.

Here is a recent YouTube screenshot of the various news anchors from stations around the US reading the same script, found on YouTube:

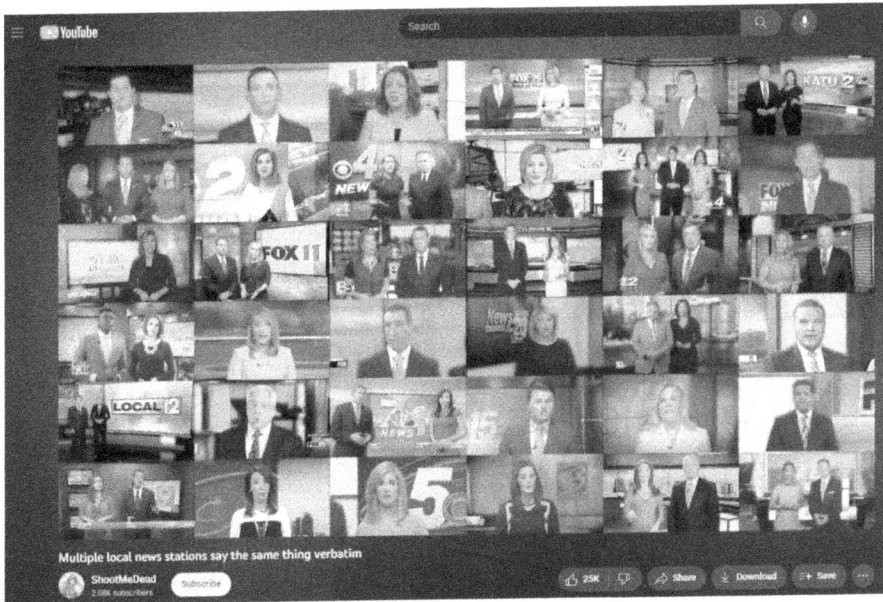

Multiple local news stations say the same thing verbatim

In recent months, however, I am starting to see a few rogue "personalities" on both sides of the aisle, who are trying to step out and be different by reporting facts based on investigative efforts and not just being a mouthpiece for the bigger Team. Granted most of these individuals have been attacked and/or removed from their positions, but nonetheless, they are taking a stance on true journalism.

Nonetheless, mainstream media has long been used as a tool for manipulation, allowing powerful entities to shape public opinion by controlling what information is presented and how it is presented. This has the potential to influence social beliefs and behavior on a large scale, giving those at the top an unprecedented level of control over the masses. In some cases, this manipulation can be subtle, such as when certain topics are given more attention than others or when facts are spun in a particular way. But in other cases, it can be far more overt: stories may be completely fabricated, or evidence might be deliberately distorted to suit an agenda. When this happens, it's easier to identify which team is motivating them.

No matter where we look—news outlets, television shows, movies—there is no denying that mainstream media manipulation exists, and its effects are far-reaching. It not only affects the way we think and act but also how laws and policies are formulated. To make matters worse, it can be difficult to identify manipulation when encountered, making us all unwitting agents in someone else's game. It is my hope that this book might make its way to some of these personalities and encourage them to shake the Versus Virus and set an example for future journalists everywhere.

Team Social Media Manipulation

Social media and search companies are also a huge part of the Versus Virus. The leaders or coaches of these teams have already decided what will and will not be shown or promoted on their platforms based on their personal beliefs and motivations. Their sole purpose is to persuade or dissuade people who are on their networks to believe or not believe information by labeling it as misinformation. And even when the story is later proven to be true, the social media or search company rarely if ever goes back to making public statements that their opinion or their decision to censor someone was wrong. These platforms utilize artificial intelligence and machine learning injected into their code that is directed to seek out and isolate any topic that has been labeled as harmful to the narrative supported by the platform. Recent examples of this have been highlighted in US House and Senate hearings pertaining to subjects such as COVID-19, vaccinations, former Presidents, and even President Biden's son.

The one example I can say that does not seem to be in this group is X (formerly known as Twitter). Elon Musk appears to genuinely be working to create a public platform that promotes open dialogue and free speech. But this effort is being attacked daily by Team Censorship. And while there are still algorithms in X that are doing harm, I believe the new team Musk has put into place has the best intentions to make this a true public forum platform for respectful discussion and dialogue of any topic. Time will tell, but I see this as a positive step towards reducing the effects of the Versus Virus.

Most of the major social media companies have been accused of manipulating the public to further their internal organizational agendas. They have been suspected of censoring certain topics, favoring certain political views, and creating echo chambers that only reinforce existing biases. The tactics listed here not only shape public opinion on important issues but also can be used to control what people see and think about. This can be dangerous, as it has the potential to create a distorted perception of reality and ultimately lead to unequal power dynamics between those in charge and those without a voice. Social media users need to stay aware of these manipulation tactics so they can make informed decisions about their interactions with these platforms. By understanding how social media companies manipulate the public, we can create a more equitable society where everyone's voice is respected.

Furthermore, it is important to recognize the power of social media platforms and hold them accountable for their actions. From my perspective, not only should governments be able to regulate these companies, but users should actively take part in holding them responsible for any manipulation tactics they may use, especially when it pertains to the censorship of free speech. This can be done by boycotting certain platforms or encouraging more transparency about user data and algorithms used by the platform. People have a right to know how their data is being used and what kind of information they are seeing online so that they can make informed decisions on which platforms to trust. By taking a stand against manipulation by social media companies, we can create an environment where everyone's voice matters regardless of background or political views.

Team Government Manipulation

Modern governments might be the largest contributors to the Versus Virus. No matter what country you visit, you see a common thread where elected government officials are working overtime to segregate the population into a divisive group of people who hate the other teams no matter what proof surfaces.

Government manipulation of voters can take many forms. It is often done through expanding or limiting access to voting, gerrymandering, and the dissemination of false information. These practices are used to influence the outcome of elections in favor of those in power, thus threatening democracy and undermining the will of citizens. In recent years, some governments have been leveraging technology to carry out these activities on a larger scale and with greater precision. Social media platforms are used to spread misinformation, personal data is collected and analyzed for voter targeting, and automated bots are deployed to amplify messages or suppress opposing views. Such actions not only violate ethical standards but also weaken the trust needed for a functioning democracy. We must remain aware of these tactics and work together to ensure that all votes are counted and respected, and that all votes are actually from people who are legally allowed to vote in that election.

We must also adopt measures to protect against future manipulation. Most can agree that governments should commit to ensuring fair and accessible elections, protecting personal data from misuse, and strengthening reporting processes for misinformation campaigns. We must take responsibility for monitoring the activities of our elected officials as well as holding them accountable if they fail to meet these standards. Ultimately, it is up to us as citizens to defend democracy by demanding transparency and fairness in our electoral process. The right to vote is a fundamental component of any healthy democratic society; we mustn't allow it to be compromised by political manipulation.

CHAPTER FIVE

TEAMS TO MOBS

When the Virus Mutates the Team into a Mob

Now that we have a good understanding of what a Team is, what teams you may personally be on, and how those teams may be manipulating you… let's take a closer look at what happens when harnessing the power of the team turns into negativity and possibly verbal and physical violence toward other people who are on different teams.

Leadership + Funding = Motivation

Every team in history has a coach and normally, a group of boosters who support the team. What is the coach's role? Who are the coaches of your teams? These are very important questions to ask yourself.

For example, if you look at political parties… who are their current leaders?

Most people will say former President Donald Trump is the leader of the Republican Party, but polls show a little less than half of the Republican Party would somewhat disagree with this. Less controversial leaders such as Ron DeSantis and Vivek Ramaswamy have recently been climbing in the polls but are still not popular enough to overtake the giant personality of Donald Trump.

While President Biden is the face of the Democratic Party, most would say its leaders, or coaches are people like Barack Obama, Hillary Clinton, Chuck Schumer and even newcomers like Alexandria Ocasio-Cortez (AOC) and her boisterous "squad."

Then you have leaders in Team Religion who have passed on long ago, but whose written teachings still drive the team forward. These are leaders such as Jesus Christ for the Christian Church, or Muhammad for Islam, or Buddha (Vishnu) for Hinduism. And since that time, powerful "church leaders" will pop up and have thousands of people who follow their teachings. Some of these people end up falling short, getting into trouble with the law, and more. I want to restress the point of not giving a person or influencer direct access to your belief system.

As an example of this, in the early 2000s, there was a mega church leader in Colorado that many people thought walked on water, including my then boss. When this leader of the Christian Mega Church was outed as a homosexual drug user, many people were devastated and brought to tears and depression. They had allowed this person to be the leader or coach of the team they held in very high regard for their personal identity, and when the leader fell, they fell as well.

In sports the role of a coach is essential to the success of any team. Coaches provide guidance, motivation, and direction to their players. They are responsible for designing strategies and tactics that take advantage of each player's strengths while minimizing weaknesses. They also help foster a sense of teamwork and camaraderie among the players, which helps create an environment conducive to peak performance. Coaches also need to have sound knowledge and understanding of the sport they are coaching to give their players the best possible advice. Lastly, coaches need to be able to communicate effectively with their team members for them to understand expectations and perform at a high level.

Ultimately, it is up to the coach to develop an effective game plan that leads to a team's success. By doing this, a coach can help their team achieve short-term and long-term goals. A good coach will also provide the necessary support and feedback needed along the way for players to reach their maximum potential. Without strong coaching, teams are unable to perform at their best or reach their highest potential. Coaches are an essential part of any successful team. They provide guidance, direction, motivation, and communication that allows for optimal performance from players and overall success for the team. Coaches have a great responsibility but also an incredible opportunity to make a difference in the lives of those they lead.

Coaches, or leaders, on the non-sport teams I have been discussing in this book also have many of the same goals and responsibilities. The problem comes in when the Teams we are talking about don't go home at the end of the night based on who scored the most points. These Teams build up animosity toward one another over time, based on the manipulation tactics I've so far mentioned, which can quickly turn a Team into a Mob.

The Coaches' Motivations Are Very Important

You must try to understand the motivations of your team coaches, as this may eventually give you the information you need to perhaps stay with your team, change teams, or simply remove yourself from a team altogether.

Let's think about a high school sports team. The coach is normally a teacher at the school, probably a former athlete themselves, and their motivation is to win the championship for the school. To win the championship, the team must win enough games to get to the playoffs and then must consistently get more points than the other teams to eventually win the championship.

Now, when we look at Political Teams, their motivation is to also win the championship for their team… which happens to be the election. Their goal is to use rhetoric and speeches, interviews, and social media posts to score enough points in public opinion to get the most points or votes at the end of the election to win the championship and control power for a set number of years. And as stated earlier… sometimes this involves manipulation.

No matter the tactics of the politician, the ultimate goal is power. Once voted into office, the politician is courted by lobbying organizations with a great deal of power and money. If the politician helps the organizations, that in turn helps the companies who fund it, and in turn, helps the politician to get rich. It is an ugly cycle that starts with employing extreme manipulation tactics onto each and every voter.

What are the Booster's role and motivations? In sports, boosters will host fundraisers to raise money for the team so the team can have uniforms, training equipment, nice facilities, and travel funds. Political donors play a significant role in the political system. By providing financial support, they can influence which candidates and causes gain traction and ultimately get elected. Donations provide individuals, organizations, and corporations with an opportunity to lend their voice to a particular issue or candidate that aligns with their beliefs and values. Through these donations, citizens can become actively involved in the political process, even if they are not able to vote or work on a campaign directly.

Furthermore, large donations can also increase access for candidates who may not have the resources available to them as well as those from marginalized communities who lack access due to systemic oppression. In this way, donor support helps elevate underrepresented voices in politics that would otherwise go unheard.

It's important to note that many other teams that I have mentioned in this book also have boosters in the form of sponsors and advertisers. Once a team takes money from a company to support their business, that sponsor is always consulted on matters of political importance. This is very evident when you research topics such as gender identity, CRT, transgender sports, and more.

From Teams to Mobs (the Difference Is Clear)

The mob mentality is what makes the Versus Virus dangerous for all of humanity. It spreads quickly and takes over the minds of everyone it touches. People become irrational, and easily influenced by the group's emotions and ideas. Before you know it, you're swept up in the chaotic tide of collective thinking—no matter how illogical or dangerous it might be. It can be a powerful force, and a dangerous one. If you ever find yourself in a large group, it's best to take a step back and remember that individual thought is always more important than the crowd. Don't let the mob mentality overtake you!

History of Mob Mentality

Mob mentality first came on the scene in the 1800s when social psychologists and groupthink pioneers Gabriel Tarde and Gustave Le Bon introduced it. In a groupthink situation, a consensus is often created from social pressures that cannot accommodate change. Since we are talking about teams, we will take the path of team think.

Being part of a team can cause a person to lose their self-awareness or experience "deindividuation." As originally stated by Tarde and Le Bon, when people deindividuate, they become less likely to follow normal social guidelines and can become more likely to lose their sense of individual identity. This can cause a person to lose their natural inhibitions, encouraging them to perform an activity they would never normally do. Their individual values and principles have been replaced by those of the team.

Frankenstein

We can even witness and watch the mob mentality visualized in older films, as I recently watched the older black and white 1931 adaptation of Mary Shelley's 1818 novel *Frankenstein*. There is a scene where an angry mob of local townspeople, armed with pitchforks and torches, set out to confront the monster and his creator over the murder of one of their own. Without fully understanding the situation, the mob gets caught up in its fears and concerns and creates a groupthink singular organism acting as one. All individual thought was completely removed.

Beauty and the Beast

In Disney's popular animated film, *Beauty and the Beast*, Gaston, who wishes to marry Belle, becomes the leader of the town, convinces the citizens that the "Beast" has kidnapped Belle, and that they must band together to destroy it at all costs. Again, the mob grabs the traditional pitchforks and torches and sets out to kill the beast without taking the time to fully understand the situation at hand.

Shrek

In *Shrek*, a young ogre sets out on his own and into the world to make his living. His parents had warned him that, because of his looks, he would be shunned by everyone, and an angry mob will be the last thing he will see before he dies. Shrek then goes on a journey to overcome the tyranny of Lord Farquaad who has banished all storybook characters to the swamps.

The Lottery

Then you have works like *The Lottery* by Stephen King or *The Purge* by James DeMonaco, which are stories that say acting out once a year with aggression will purge your desire for violence and anger the rest of the year. Acting out with aggression may seem like it would lead to emotional relief, but the reality is, and many experts agree, that acting out our rage is more likely to increase aggression than purge it.

What we see in the modern-day regarding mob mentality is the burning of cities, looting of businesses, and the occupation of the White House itself.

Violence and threats in the modern day (against both political parties) are quickly becoming the norm.

Examples of How Mob Mentality Is Harmful to Society

In recent years, there have been numerous examples of modern-day riots around the world. In 2020, protests in response to the death of George Floyd turned violent in cities like Minneapolis, Chicago, Los Angeles, and Atlanta across the United States. There were reports of widespread looting and property damage as some protestors clashed with police officers. Similarly, demonstrations against police brutality following the killing of Breonna Taylor also led to violence in Louisville, Kentucky.

Elsewhere, Hong Kong was rocked by riots throughout 2019 and into 2020 as citizens protested a proposed extradition law that would allow people living in Hong Kong to be sent to mainland China for trial. The protests quickly escalated into clashes between protesters and security forces outside government buildings.

More recently, mass demonstrations against controversial reforms to Chile's pension system turned violent in the city of Santiago. Protestors set up barricades, looted shops, and clashed with security forces resulting in injuries, arrests, and millions of dollars' worth of damage.

The examples above demonstrate how quickly seemingly peaceful demonstrations can turn into chaotic and destructive riots if not handled carefully. Governments must find ways to address the concerns of their citizens without resorting to violence. Unfortunately, this is often easier said than done.

When it comes to handling large-scale demonstrations, communication and dialogue are key. Governments must be willing to listen to protestors' grievances and work with them toward a resolution rather than escalating the situation through force or aggression. Strict adherence to international standards of human rights and the rule of law is also essential.

Ultimately, it is up to governments to ensure that protests remain peaceful and do not lead to rioting. It is only through careful management of public demonstrations that riots can be avoided in the future.

Riots Versus Protests

When you do a simple search on any leading search engine for the phrase "violence versus protests," the overwhelming first page results are from Liberal-leaning organizations stating that the new protest involves some sort of violence. As a tech guy myself who has built several tech businesses, I understand that search engine results are fluid for the most part. However, there is a reason that search engines, along with social media companies, have been taken before Congress and questioned over the past two years pertaining to their "unbiased search results." Again, this goes back to the idea that being on Team Search Engine is probably not a good idea as their coach seemingly works to per-suade you to be on a specific team or set of teams that align with their own corporate beliefs. As a researcher and the author of this book, I believe that a public search engine should do a better job at showing both sides of the story to allow you to use more of your critical thinking skills to decide for yourself. This leading search engine undoubtedly has great technology, but the Versus Virus seems to have infected their search results on multiple high-profile topics, which again, only in my opinion, could be enhancing underlying mental health issues to users. And if this is too big of a leap for you, I encourage you to do your own research into search engine bias.

This is exactly what I am talking about when I say that the teams you choose are working overtime to control your thoughts and behaviors. This also opens the door to advocate for major search engines to be held accountable for generating search results that can negatively impact the mental health of its users. I do not mean they should be held accountable to one team or another, but held accountable to the impacts of mental health on humanity.

Violence Versus Communicating

This point needs some time and thought.

As an example, I want you to consider two Teams on a playing field. Each has the desire to win the challenge by gaining power over the other. Two main tactics can be used here: violence and communication.

Violence is used to overpower your opponent physically,

rendering them weakened and sometimes injured. When your opponent can't fight back, you win the challenge and assert your power over the others. But have you solved anything? Or have you simply created a group that resents you even more and will be working overtime behind the scenes to build up their forces to the point they can physically overpower you? This results in an endless cycle of destruction and animosity. This type of play works in sports because the goal is to overpower your opponent and score more points. But in life, this approach to conflict is unhealthy and can end up in harmful and lasting results.

Communication, on the other hand, is a more elevated or enlightened form of debate that gives respect to each side's wants, needs, feelings, and emotions. The idea of communicating is to get to an agreement that benefits both sides of the argument. One side may eventually win more of what they wanted, but the resentment is minimal and both sides appear to be working together for a common goal. In my area of expertise, this is referred to as "effective communication."

The Versus Virus has seemingly forced the majority of the population to favor violence over communication. Just like the search I did earlier, this team, and the teams that the search engine is promoting, are telling readers that violence is necessary to get what you want politically. That is a major factor when turning on the news and seeing cities being burned down, groups of people being tear-gassed, businesses being looted, regular citizens being attacked on the streets, and random people walking into schools, clubs, and shopping centers and opening fire on strangers. These "Search Teams" need to take responsibility for what they are showing and reporting to people as they can be viewed as a catalyst in much of this activity.

However, the flip side of this argument goes back to free speech. Is it a search engine's duty to filter or limit the freedom of certain websites to be listed as an option in a general search? I want to make sure you are always looking at both sides of the argument and both potential teams in the debate.

Let's do a self-evaluation.

Start by circling which of the teams you believe you are on, based on the topics discussed in this book.

Team Liberal	Team Conservative
Team Left Wing	Team Right Wing
Team Woke	Team Anti-Woke
Team Pro-Choice	Team Pro-Life
Team Gun Control	Team 2nd Amendment
Team Patriotism	Team Anti-Patriotism
Team Atheist	Team Religion
Team Black	Team White
Team Electric	Team Fossil Fuel
Team Vax	Team Choice
Team Censorship	Team Free Speech
Team School Policy	Team School Choice
Team Transgender Athlete	Team Women's Sports

Who is coaching or leading each team that you circled? Who are the highest-profile leaders of each team that you believe you are on? Take time to research the leaders of each team you circled in the previous section.

Teams You Circled	Their Coach or Leader

Next, write one short line that represents what each of the teams you are on stands for.

1 _____

2 _____

3 _____

4 _____

5 _____

6 _____

7 _____

8 _____

9 _____

10 _____

11 _____

12 _____

13 _____

Have any of the leaders or coaches on your teams ever promoted violence over communication? Be careful… leaders on both sides of the political aisle have done this. Especially when you are thinking of political topics such as abortion, gun control and more.

Political leaders have a responsibility to promote peace and peaceful means of resolving conflict. Unfortunately, in some cases, they have been known to incite violence or endorse violent solutions instead. For example, during the Rwandan genocide of 1994, Hutu Power political leaders called on their followers to commit acts of ethnic cleansing against Tutsis and moderate Hutus. Similarly, in 2019 Brazilian President Jair Bolsonaro instigated Brazilians to use violence against Indigenous groups for taking up arms against illegal loggers on their ancestral land.

Then in the United States, you have multiple video montages circulating of Democratic political leaders calling on members of the Liberal Team to go out and "get in their faces" and "make them suffer." And you have influencers from the same team talking about assassination and blowing up the White House.

And on the other side, there is the controversy of the January 6th, 2021 "insurrection" of the White House that was allegedly promoted by Republican leadership.

In my humble opinion, when a coach promotes violence to their team, it may be time to exit the team or to put a new coach in place.

CHAPTER SIX

THE NEED TO BELONG TO A GROUP

Now that we understand the difference between teams and mobs, let's take a step back. Why do we fall prey, lose our own identity, and take on that of a group?

Maslow Hierarchy, Sense of Belonging

It's no surprise that feeling a sense of belonging is important to us as humans. As Abraham Maslow once said, "The need for interpersonal relationships and love lie at the heart of our being." While we may feel most comfortable in the company of friends and family, it's also possible to find a sense of belonging anywhere. Whether it's a particular place of worship, your favorite cafe, a gym, or workout class, or even an online community, the sense of connection and belonging can be found anywhere that resonates with us.

Sense of Belonging

A sense of belonging does not depend on participation with, or proximity to, others or groups. Rather, belonging comes from a perception of quality, meaning, and satisfaction with social connections. Belonging may also relate to a sense of belonging to a place or even an event.

From a sociological standpoint, "the sense of belonging and identification involves the feeling, belief, and expectation that one fits in the group and has a place there, a feeling of acceptance by the group, and a willingness to sacrifice for the group." (McMillan, D. W., & Chavis, D. M. [1986]. Sense of community: A definition and theory. (*Journal of Community Psychology*) This quote is from actual published researchers to show you that I believe the sense of belonging is very important as it pertains to the Versus Virus.

Study after study has found a strong positive correlation between a sense of belonging and the meaningfulness of life. Though most things I have read seem to refer to "the desire for social connections with both people and people in a group" instead of a sense of belonging.

CHAPTER 7

HOW TO BE VIRUS FREE

ELIMINATING THE VERSUS VIRUS IN YOUR LIFE

Rise Above the Noise: 5 Steps to Becoming Enlightened and Free of the Versus Virus

We now have a thorough understanding of what I have identified as the Versus Virus. We also have a better understanding of the teams you are on and the manipulation tactics they may be using to control your thoughts and behaviors. We then built a general understanding of how teams can turn into mobs, and how all of this relates to a general sense of belonging that is an innate need in every human. We have built a pretty solid foundation that outlines how the Versus Virus may be impacting your life and your relationships.

Now let's look at the five simple steps I have outlined to help you rid your mind and body of this virus.

STEP 1: Get Your Mental Health In Order

We cannot separate the importance of a sense of belonging from our physical and mental health. The social ties that accompany a sense of belonging are a protective factor helping manage stress and other behavioral issues. When we feel we have support and are not alone, we are more resilient, often coping more effectively with difficult times in our lives. Coping well with hardships decreases the physical and mental effects of these situations.

We begin life with the most crucial of needs—attachment to a caregiver. This is the beginning of our fundamental need for belonging. Studies have shown that children who have not achieved a healthy attachment in their young lives have lower self-esteem, a more negative worldview, are mistrustful, and can have a perception of rejection.

Depression, anxiety, and suicidal ideation are common mental health conditions associated with lacking a sense of belonging. These conditions can lead to social behaviors that interfere with a person's ability to connect to others, creating a cycle of events that further weakens a sense of belonging.

Gratefully, we do have control in making changes in our lives to break this cycle and bolster our sense of belonging.

Mental health is a crucial component of overall wellness, and it should not be taken lightly. Mental illness can range from mild symptoms to severe, debilitating conditions that can significantly impact one's ability to function in daily life. Therefore, individuals need to take steps toward maintaining their mental health so they can lead happy, healthy lives. Such steps may include engaging in regular physical activity, getting enough sleep and rest, managing stress, pursuing meaningful activities or hobbies, eating a balanced diet, limiting alcohol intake, and talking to a mental health professional if needed.

Taking the initiative to prioritize one's emotional well-being is essential for long-term health and happiness. It can be hard to take the first step towards improving one's mental health, but it is an essential part of a healthy lifestyle. Taking care of your mental health should be taken as seriously as taking care of your physical health. Making yourself a priority and investing in your mental well-being could make all the difference in how you feel today and for years to come. Everyone deserves to live their best life and taking the steps necessary to do that starts with honoring our mental health.

STEP 2: Enhance Your Critical Thinking Skills

Critical thinking is self-guided, self-disciplined thinking which attempts to reason at the highest level of quality in a fair-minded way.

Improving your critical thinking skills can help you to better analyze and evaluate information, come up with creative solutions to problems, and make more informed decisions. It is an essential skill for success in many areas of life.

One way to enhance your critical thinking skills is to practice asking questions. Ask yourself "why" a certain piece of information might be important or what insight it provides about the issue at hand. Also, ask yourself if there are any potential biases involved in the presentation of the data... is this a manipulation tactic? By questioning things as you go along, you'll be able to get a deeper understanding of the topic at hand and form stronger opinions about it.

Another way to improve your critical thinking capabilities is to learn how to recognize various kinds of logical fallacies. Logical fallacies are statements that appear to be true but contain errors in their reasoning. Being able to spot these fallacies can help you sort out facts from fiction and make sounder decisions.

A logical fallacy is an error in reasoning that renders an argument invalid. Logical fallacies occur when someone uses faulty logic, incorrect assumptions, or misleading statements to draw a conclusion. They are often used by people who want to win an argument without having the facts on their side.

Examples of common logical fallacies include ad hominem attacks, false dichotomies, non sequiturs, and appeals to emotion. The key is to identify these fallacies in order to avoid making the same mistakes yourself. By understanding logical fallacies and recognizing them when you hear them, you can be a more informed consumer of information. As such, it is essential that everyone exercises critical thinking skills when evaluating arguments. Doing so can help ensure that you are making decisions based on fact rather than emotion or faulty logic.

Finally, practice listening actively when engaging in conversations or debates with others. Instead of just hearing what someone is saying, try to understand the meaning behind it and consider how your own opinions might have been influenced by the other person's point of view. Doing this will help you develop more complex thinking skills as well as enhance your understanding of different perspectives on topics.

By making a conscious effort to improve your critical thinking skills, you can become a better problem-solver and decision-maker. Taking the time to hone your ability to think critically can also pay dividends in both your professional and personal life.

STEP 3: Understand the Motivations of the Teams You Are a Part Of

Understanding others' motivations can be critical when it comes to relationships, work projects, and teams. Motivations are driven by an individual's unique blend of values, beliefs, needs, and desires. Identifying what motivates someone else can help you see things from their perspective and build a better relationship or come up with a better plan for achieving success on a project.

There are several ways to identify the motivations of yourself or someone else. Firstly, look at the person's body language and watch how they respond in different situations. Pay attention to their facial expressions and vocal tone as these can give clues as to their underlying emotions and thoughts. Secondly, observe their behavior—what do they consistently say yes to? What do they avoid? Thirdly, ask questions. Ask yourself or the other person what values and beliefs are important to them. What do they hope to get out of a particular situation or relationship?

Ultimately, understanding others' motivations can be a powerful tool for creating strong connections and achieving collective success. With careful observation and communication, you can identify and work with the underlying motivation that drives different people in different ways. In doing so, you will develop an invaluable skill—one which will serve you in many situations throughout life.

STEP 4: Evaluate Your Beliefs and Where They Came From (Ethnocentrism)

When it comes to evaluating your beliefs, it is important to think deeply about them and consider the implications of holding onto belief. Take some time to reflect on what you believe and why you believe it, and then ask yourself if this belief still holds true in today's world. If not, other perspectives could help inform various angles and be open-minded when considering new ideas. Also, ask yourself if your beliefs can be backed up by facts or scientific evidence. This process of self-reflection can help you understand why you have certain beliefs and provide insight into how you might adjust them for a better understanding of the world around us. Ultimately, understanding and reevaluating our beliefs can help us become better informed and more open-minded individuals.

In addition to reflective thinking, it is important to seek out varying perspectives as part of evaluating your beliefs. Look for sources that provide different points of view on the topics you're interested in, being sure to take into account any potential biases they may hold. This can be done by researching other opinions and reading up on related topics, or even discussing them with friends and family who have a different viewpoint than yours. Doing so can help broaden your understanding of various issues and allow you to develop a more holistic perspective.

Overall, taking time to evaluate your beliefs is an important step toward becoming a knowledgeable individual. It allows you to understand why you believe certain things and consider the opinions of others. Be sure to be open-minded when examining different perspectives, as this can help you develop an informed perspective on various topics. By taking the time to evaluate your beliefs, you can make sure that you are bettering yourself and making informed decisions about the world around us.

It's also important to me that we address the concept of ethnocentrism here. Ethnocentrism, "the attitude that one's own group, ethnicity, or nationality is superior to others" as described by the Merriam-Webster Dictionary, can have a powerful and lasting effect on how people interact with one another, as well as how they view themselves and the world around them. It can lead to an "us versus them" mentality that prevents individuals from considering different perspectives or cultures. This mindset can cause people to judge, stereotype, and even discriminate against those who are perceived as different, perpetuating intolerance, and creating divisions within societies. Ethnocentrism also has far-reaching consequences, such as influencing public policy decisions, international conflicts, and economic disparities. Ultimately, ethnocentrism creates an environment of exclusion rather than inclusion—one in which it is nearly impossible for diverse groups to coexist peacefully. To create positive change in the world, it is essential to move away from this mentality and instead foster understanding and acceptance. By learning about other cultures, challenging our own biases, and embracing diversity, we can work together to build a better future for all.

This was one of the major driving forces behind the creation of my current company, Huvr. I wanted to build a tool that gave anyone the ability to travel the world virtually and in real-time and see new things, talk to new people, and research on their own, without the influence and manipulation of teams.

STEP 5: Educate Yourself Constantly–Never Stop

I am a lifelong student of the humanities and the physical sciences. The antidote to the Versus Virus is education: understanding how teams operate and being aware of potential areas of manipulation will go a long way towards combating its influence. Ultimately, it is up to us as individuals to become more conscious consumers of news and entertainment and to recognize when we may be subjected to manipulative tactics. Only then can we begin to combat the insidious power of team manipulation and eradicate the Versus Virus once and for all.

Remember…

It's okay to adjust your belief system as more information comes to light.

Learn to research on your own and make certain you are looking at all viewpoints before making an informed decision.

Learn to communicate with empathy and logic. (Good emotion versus bad emotion.) After all, it's our ability to connect to others through verbal and nonverbal communication that makes us all human in the end.

Your individual freedom and your individuality are the greatest gift you have been given in this life. And I hope that after reading this book, you start the process of understanding what teams you are on, what teams are potentially manipulating your thoughts and behaviors, and, if you so choose, you have the strength to make the conscious choice to remove yourself from these teams and live your life free from the Versus Virus.

Individuality is a gift that should be cherished and cel-ebrated, not suppressed or discouraged. We are all unique and have something special to bring to the world. There is no one else out there just like you; your thoughts, ideas, and perspectives matter. Embrace who you are and express it fearlessly. You will make a difference in this world if you stand up for yourself and be proud of who you are instead of trying to fit into someone else's idea of perfection. Make your voice heard! You will find that when you shine your light, others will follow suit. Celebrate your individuality—it is an irreplaceable part of what makes you wonderful.

Herman has spent his career at the apex of creative content creation, business development, and technology.

He is a decorated veteran of the Gulf War where he honorably served in the US Air Force. While there, he earned the National Defense Service Medal for his participation in the Gulf War and was a member recipient of the Presidential Unit Citation for his activities in the Green Ramp Disaster at Pope Air Force Base. Following active duty, Herman returned to college where he worked to complete his bachelor's, master's, and Ph.D. During this time, Herman also continued working as a civilian in the United States government where he held titles such as Program Manager III working directly with the Centers for Disease Control, Chief of Communications and Director of Technology.

After thirteen years in senior-level government managing multi-million-dollar budgets for state and federal agencies, he took his talents to the private business world.

Along the way he has tallied some major accomplishments. From album and video creation with major and former #1 music artists to filing patents on major technology products that ended in M&A, to partnerships with major Big Box Retailers such as Target and Best Buy, Herman has proven his ability to take an idea from thought to fully executed business.

In addition, Herman has run original idea companies that were nationally distributed. He led one of the largest music distribution companies in the early 2000s where he personally secured contracts with Sony, Warner, Universal, EMI Capital Records and more. Herman has always sought out and excelled at challenges in the business world.

In 2019, Herman founded his latest company, Huvr. Huvr develops technology that gives a user virtual access to mobile locations and virtual events around the world without them physically being there. He is currently working towards the goal of connecting the world like never before and combatting the effects of ethnocentricity and poverty.

Published by
TVGUESTPERT PUBLISHING

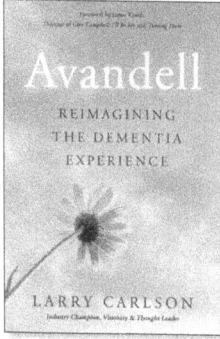

LARRY CARLSON
Avandell: Reimagining the Dementia Experience
Hardcover: $17.95
Kindle: $9.99

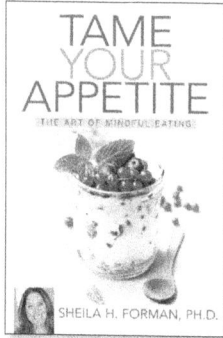

SHEILA H. FORMAN, Ph.D
Tame Your Appetite: The Art of Mindful Eating
Paperback: $16.95
Kindle: $9.99

SHEILA H. FORMAN, Ph.D
Mindful Bite, Joyful Life: 365 Days of Mindful Eating
Paperback: $22.95
Kindle: $9.99

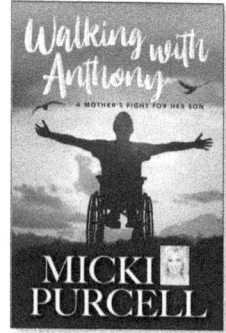

MICKI PURCELL
Walking With Anthony: A Mother's Fight For Her Son
Hardcover $22.95
Kindle: $9.99

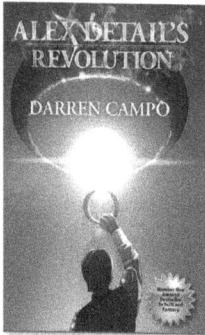

DARREN CAMPO
Alex Detail's Revolution
Paperback: $9.95
Hardcover: $22.95
Kindle: $9.15

DARREN CAMPO
Alex Detail's Rebellion
Hardcover: $22.95
Kindle: $9.99

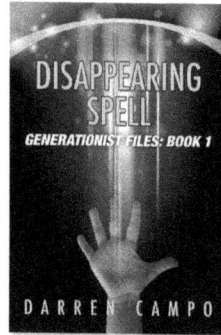

DARREN CAMPO
Disappearing Spell: Generationist Files: Book 1
Kindle: $2.99

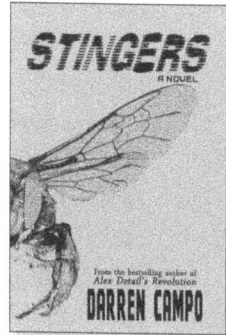

DARREN CAMPO
Stingers
Paperback: $9.99
Kindle: $9.99

TVGuestpert Publishing
11664 National Blvd, #345
Los Angeles, CA. 90064
310-584-1504
www.TVGPublishing.com

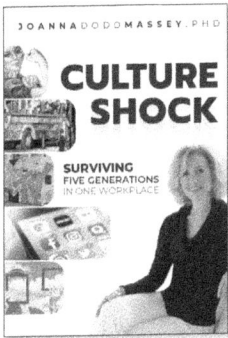

JOANNA DODD MASSEY
Culture Shock: Surviving Five Generations in One Workplace
Paperback: $16.95
Kindle/Nook: $9.99

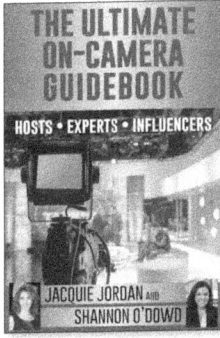

JACQUIE JORDAN AND SHANNON O'DOWD
*The Ultimate On-Camera Guidebook: Hosts*Experts*Influencers*
Paperback: $16.95
Kindle: $9.99

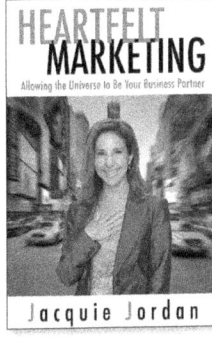

JACQUIE JORDAN
Heartfelt Marketing: Allowing the Universe to Be Your Business Partner
Paperback: $15.95
Kindle: $9.99
Audible: $9.95

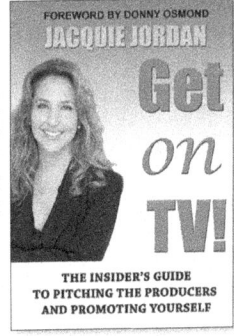

JACQUIE JORDAN
Get on TV! The Insider's Guide to Pitching the Producers and Promoting Yourself
Published by Sourcebooks
Paperback: $14.95
Kindle: $9.99
Nook: $14.95

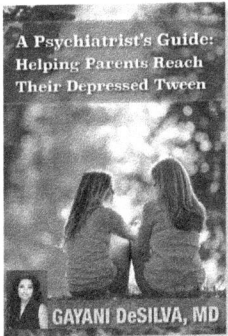

GAYANI DESILVA, MD
A Psychiatrist's Guide: Helping Parents Reach Their Depressed Tween
Paperback: $16.95
Kindle: $9.99

GAYANI DESILVA, MD
A Psychiatrist's Guide: Stop Teen Addiction Before It Starts
Paperback: $16.95
Kindle: $9.99
Audible: $14.95

JACK H. HARRIS
Father of the Blob: The Making of a Monster Smash and Other Hollywood Tales
Paperback: $16.95
Kindle/Nook: $9.99

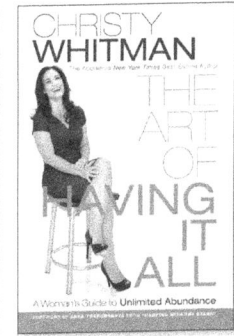

New York Times Best Seller
CHRISTY WHITMAN
The Art of Having It All: A Woman's Guide to Unlimited Abundance
Paperback: $16.95
Kindle/Nook: $9.99
Audible Book: $13.00

Published by
TVGUESTPERT PUBLISHING

TVGuestpert Publishing
11664 National Blvd, #345
Los Angeles, CA. 90064
310-584-1504
www.TVGPublishing.com

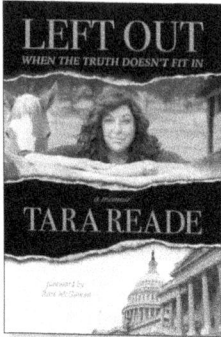

TARA READE
Left Out: When The Truth Doesn't Fit In
Hardcover: $22.95
Paperback: $19.95
Kindle: $9.99

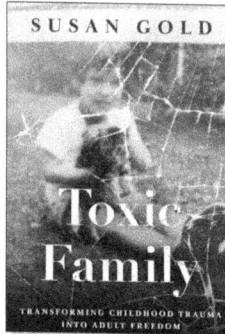

SUSAN GOLD
Toxic Family: Transforming Childhood Trauma into Adult Freedom
Paperback: $19.95
Kindle: $9.99

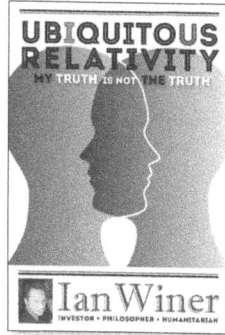

IAN WINER
Ubiquitous Relativity: My Truth is Not the Truth
Paperback: $16.95
Kindle: $9.99

www.ingramcontent.com/pod-product-compliance
Lightning Source LLC
Chambersburg PA
CBHW022130280326
41933CB00007B/626